Sand
publis
writter
puzzle
anima
She n
husbar
two ca

Sally
books
the *Ind*
robots and has a daughter called Emerald

the
science
of...

SPYMAKER
SPYING
HANDBOOK

SANDY RANSFORD

Illustrated by Sally Kindberg

MACMILLAN CHILDREN'S BOOKS

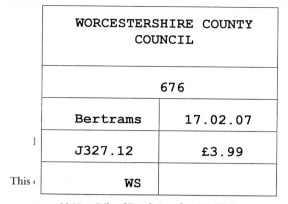

20 New Wharf Road, London N1 9RR
Basingstoke and Oxford
www.panmacmillan.com

Associated companies throughout the world

ISBN: 978-0-330-44957-1

1 3 5 7 9 8 6 4 2

A CIP catalogue record for this book is available from
the British Library.

Typeset by Nigel Hazle
Printed and bound in Great Britain by Mackays of Chatham plc, Kent

CONTENTS

cut
out

INTRODUCTION

Do you know what a secret agent is? A secret agent, or spy, is someone who finds out their enemy's secrets, by going into the enemy's camp and watching what is going on, by checking and reporting on the movements of enemy agents, by finding and reading secret documents and computer files and then reporting their finds back to headquarters.

The most famous spy in the world is probably James Bond, who, of course, was not a real spy but a fictional one created by Ian Fleming. But he is the person who comes into the minds of most of us when we think about spies and secret agents. It seems like an action-packed life of glamour, danger and excitement. Real-life spying isn't much like that. Real-life spies often have to spend many lonely hours in uncomfortable places watching what goes on. Far from meeting exotic girls and eating and drinking in expensive restaurants and casinos, they may go hungry because they cannot desert their post.

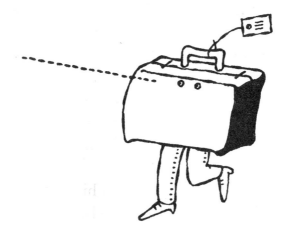

Not all spying is political. Industrial spies check out what their competitors are producing. Sometimes a spy employed by one company will go to work for another specifically to find out their secrets and report back to their original employer. A spy 'planted' to operate in this way is called a 'mole'. There are even spies whose job it is to find out about the diet and exercise routines of top sportsmen and women.

Whatever the spy's job, he or she needs to know how to observe without being seen, how to pass information to another without being suspected, how to disguise their appearance so they won't be recognized, how to follow someone without being spotted, how to hide their equipment so no one will find it – plus a host of other things. And if you want to learn how to be a secret agent, you need to learn all these things too. You don't need to look too far. Here, within the pages of *The Secret Agent's Handbook*, you will find everything you need to know to set you up as a spy. Who and what you spy on is up to you. Once word gets round that you are a highly trained agent, people will be queueing up to use your services. Good luck!

P.S. A secret agent has to keep his or her brain razor-sharp at all times – spies live by their wits. So just to help you keep up to the mark, at the end of each chapter there is a short quiz or puzzle to test your knowledge and your brain power.

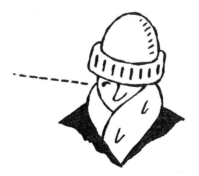

REAL-LIFE SPY ORGANIZATIONS AND FAMOUS SPIES

Spies have been around for a long time. The very first spy organization in Britain was formed in the sixteenth century by Queen Elizabeth I's Secretary of State, Sir Francis Walsingham.

SPY ORGANIZATIONS

MI5

MI5 was set up in 1909 to seek out and identify German spies operating in Britain. Its name means 'military intelligence, section five', and it is responsible for the security of the UK, and for counter-intelligence. Its agents investigate people and organizations that they believe may threaten national security, though unlike the police they do not have the power to arrest people.

MI6

MI6, or 'military intelligence, section six', was originally called the Secret Intelligence Service. It is concerned with foreign intelligence and works as part of the Foreign Office. During the 1930s and 1940s, MI6 was considered the most effective intelligence service in the world, but it was later discovered that it had been penetrated by Soviet agents since the 1930s (see below). MI6 is the agency that issues 'D notices' under the Official Secrets Act, forbidding newspapers from publishing anything it considers may be harmful to Britain's security.

CIA

The CIA – Central Intelligence Agency – is the USA's intelligence and counter-intelligence service. It was created in 1947. It is divided into four main parts. The Intelligence Directorate analyses material which has been gathered by the agency's spies. The Directorate of Operations organizes the spies and their activities. The Directorate of Science and Technology keeps its people up to date with the latest scientific advances and develops technical devices to aid their work (just like the scientific officer in the Bond films). The fourth division is the Administration Directorate.

The CIA's work can be controversial – it became involved in illegal operations in the Watergate scandal which brought down President Nixon.

KGB

These initials stand for *Komitet Gosudarstvennoy Bezopasnosti*, which means the Committee for State Security, and the KGB was the intelligence and counter-intelligence service of the former Soviet Union (Russia and some surrounding states). It also performed duties within the Union. These included providing protection for political leaders, supervising the country's borders, censorship of the media and the arts and controlling travel to and from the USSR both by its own citizens and by foreign visitors. Since the USSR broke up into separate states, the KGB has been succeeded by the FSB, or Federal Security Service.

FAMOUS SPIES

Mata Hari

Born in 1876, Mata Hari was a glamorous Dutch/Indonesian nightclub dancer who joined the German secret service – possibly as early as 1907. She mixed with high-ranking military and government officers on both the German and Allied sides in the First World War, and passed on the Allies' military secrets to the Germans. Her activities were found out by the French, who executed her in Paris in 1917.

Lord Baden-Powell

Famous for founding the Boy Scout movement in 1908, Lord Baden-Powell also spied for Britain during the First World War. Pretending to be a scientist studying insects, he drew detailed drawings of butterflies, and hid plans of enemy fortifications in the design of their wings.

Burgess and MacLean

Guy Burgess worked for the BBC, wrote propaganda material for Britain in the Second World War and was recruited by MI5. He also worked for the Foreign Office, and was appointed Second Secretary in Washington in 1950. However, what his employers did not know was that he had been an undercover agent for the Soviet Union since the 1930s.

Donald MacLean was the son of a Liberal cabinet minister who worked in the Diplomatic Service in the 1930s and 1940s, but from 1944 was actually a Soviet agent. Burgess and MacLean were part of a spy ring recruited at Cambridge University. MacLean became head of the American Department of the Foreign Office, but gradually people began to suspect that he was not quite what he appeared to be. By this time Guy Burgess was also under suspicion, and he was recalled from the USA in 1951. Before the authorities could detain them, both Burgess and MacLean fled to Russia in 1951, where they lived for the rest of their lives.

Anthony Blunt

Anthony Blunt was a very distinguished art historian, who held the important office of

Surveyor of the Queen's Pictures from 1945 to 1972 and was awarded a knighthood. He worked for British Intelligence during the Second World War, but at the same time he was secretly employed as a Soviet spy, passing on information to the Russians. He also helped to recruit spies by informing the USSR about people in Britain who were likely to be sympathetic to communist ideas, and who might therefore become useful agents. He was stripped of his knighthood in 1979.

Helen and Peter Kroger

In the 1960s, this quiet, middle-aged couple who lived in a bungalow in a London suburb were discovered to be highly professional Soviet spies. Under the floorboards of their very ordinary, anonymous-looking home was found a hoard of spying equipment, including radio apparatus, cameras, photographic materials, and a microdot reader which was hidden in a tin of talcum powder.

HOW TO DISGUISE YOURSELF

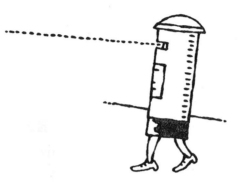

CREATING A NEW IDENTITY

If you want to become a secret agent, you must first create a new identity for yourself. Real agents, travelling in foreign countries, often pretend to be businessmen selling or buying products abroad. This gives them the opportunity to visit companies' headquarters and meet people who may be spy contacts. No one suspects who they really are. You can do the same. Think up a name – nothing too exotic, or people might be suspicious – an occupation and an address. So, for example, instead of being Joe Taylor, schoolboy, of 23 Rylands Avenue, Wolverhampton, you become

John Turner, engineer, of 75 Holbrook Road, Wimbledon, London. It is useful to keep the same initials in case they appear on any of your belongings. If they were different from those of your assumed name they would give the game away. If you use email, change your email address when you change your identity. When you are working as an agent, disguise yourself so your appearance matches your new identity.

CHANGING YOUR APPEARANCE

It is best if an agent is not recognized by anyone who sees him or her. With a bit of ingenuity, you can make yourself look completely different.

Body padding

To make yourself look fatter, strap a cushion or a pillow round your middle, under your clothes. You will need to borrow some larger, loose clothes to go over it. Roll up a towel, secure it with string or elastic bands, and put that across your shoulders to give you a hunched look and make you look taller. A large,

look fatter

old raincoat is ideal to wrap round yourself to hide any padding underneath. You could attach the padding to the inside of the raincoat, so if you need to become yourself again very quickly you can simply take off the coat.

Looking taller

If you are a girl it is easy to make yourself look taller as you can wear a pair of high-heeled shoes or boots. Be sure to practise walking in them at home before you wear them for spying. It can take a while to learn how to do it! If you are a boy, you may be able to find shoes or boots with higher heels than your usual shoes. Even a centimetre or so can make a difference. And if you want to look taller, you need to hold yourself up very straight when you walk. This can make quite a difference.

practise walking

Looking smaller

This is more difficult, but if you round your shoulders and walk rather bent, you will appear to be smaller. You could pretend to be old and walk with a stick.

pretend to
be old

Disguising the way you move

If you are the kind of person who walks briskly and does things quickly, slow down. Walk with slow, ponderous steps and be slow and clumsy in your actions. On the other hand, if you move slowly, practise being brisk!

To give yourself a stiff leg and make you walk

with a limp, wrap some cotton wool round a ruler and tie it to the back of your knee with a scarf or a large handkerchief. It will be hidden by your trousers. Or put a pebble in your shoe to make you walk with a genuine limp. If you just pretend, you are bound to forget which is your bad leg, or you might just forget to limp altogether!

pebble

Right-handed or left?

If you know you are going to be watched closely, practise being right-handed if you are normally left-handed, and vice versa. It is not an easy thing to do, and it may be best to avoid writing unless you are sure you can manage it.

Girl or boy?

To make yourself appear to be a member of the opposite sex you need to wear the right kind of clothing and alter your hair and face (see pages 17–21). Walk with longer strides to look more like a boy; with shorter strides to look more like a girl.

←boy→

Girls' clothes fasten with the right-hand side wrapped over the left; boys' clothes fasten with the left wrapped over the right. If you have a large, old raincoat, wrap it the opposite way round if you want to pretend to be of the opposite sex. If the buttons won't fasten, then just tie a belt round your waist. Take care that enemy agents do not notice your hands. Hands are a real giveaway – boys' hands are usually larger and stronger-looking than girls'.

Disguising your voice

You can simply try to speak in a lower or higher tone of voice, or, if you are a good mimic, try to copy a regional accent. But here are some other ways you can change the sound of your voice. Of course, you can only do some of them if you are speaking over the phone and cannot be seen!

1. Hold the end of your nose between your thumb and first finger, and you will sound as if you have a heavy cold.

Heddo!

2. Press your tongue against your lower front teeth. You will speak with a lisp.
3. Put a handkerchief over the telephone receiver and speak through it.
4. Speak with a finger or thumb in your mouth.
5. Tuck a small, sausage-shaped piece of foam rubber, or a rolled-up cotton handkerchief, into one cheek down by your lower back teeth. (This is also a good way of changing the appearance of your face, but then you will need a roll on each side.)
6. Tie a scarf or large handkerchief over your nose and mouth, bandit-fashion.

disguise your voice

Changing your face

If you can borrow some make-up you can have a great time making yourself look completely different. But even if you have no make-up you can achieve good results using talcum powder to make you look paler, or cocoa powder to make you look tanned. Grey eyeshadow or eyeliner pencil rubbed across the lower part of your cheeks, chin and upper lip will make you look like a man in need of a shave.

To make yourself look older

1. Look at yourself in the mirror and frown really hard.
2. Where your face wrinkles, draw in lines, either with the cocoa powder and a small paintbrush, or, if you can borrow or buy one, an eyebrow or eyeliner pencil. Or you could use grey eyeshadow and paint it on with a narrow brush.
3. With your finger rub a little grey eyeshadow under your eyes to give you dark shadows.
4. Brush a little talcum powder on to your eyebrows and on to your hair at the temples to make it look as if you are going grey.

Changing your hairstyle

You can do this in a number of ways and end up looking completely different.

1. If you have long hair, tie it back, plait it, or push it all under a hat or cap.
2. Change your parting from one side to another, or to the centre.
3. If you have a fringe, brush all your hair back. If you don't have a fringe, brush your hair forwards to give yourself one.
4. If you are a girl, try using different hairgrips or slides to pin back part of your hair.
5. If your hair is difficult to keep in place, comb it out with a wet comb, or borrow some hairspray to keep it where you want it.

Using props

1. A scarf. Tie it round your neck, round your head or round your waist to create a number of different effects.
2. A hat. You can pull it well down to hide most of your face, tuck all your hair underneath it, wear it on the side of your head or tilt it backwards. You might decorate it with a ribbon, a bunch of flowers or a badge, and you can turn the brim up or down.

3. Dark glasses. A large pair of sunglasses is a marvellous disguise as they hide most of your face. If you want to look sinister and make people feel uncomfortable, buy a pair with reflecting lenses.

4. False hair. You can buy wigs, false moustaches and beards in a variety of styles and colours and have a lot of fun creating different effects with them. Proper wigs are expensive, but joke shops often sell crêpe 'hair' which is much cheaper, and which you can use to create beards, moustaches, sideburns and even bushy eyebrows. (See 'How to make a false beard', below.)

5. Plasticine. You can make a false nose with a lump of Plasticine. Roll it round in your hand to make it soft and pliable, then mould it into the shape you want and place it over your own nose. Check the effect in the mirror. When you have got the shape you want, press it hard on to your nose and spread make-up and face powder over it to make it blend in.

false

6. Teeth. You can buy odd-looking teeth to wear over

your own at a joke shop. If you can find a theatrical supplies shop, you can buy special paint to discolour or black out your teeth. You must not use these on capped teeth, however.

7. Scars. You can create a scar by using a product called collodion, which you can buy at a theatrical suppliers. You simply paint it on to your skin with the brush provided. As the collodion dries it contracts, puckering the skin up to form a scar. Dab a little face powder on top of it to hide any shine. Do not use it near your eyes, on broken skin, or if you have sensitive skin.

How to Make a False Beard and Moustache

You will need
Some string
Some cotton wool or crêpe hair
A pair of scissors
Some glue
Some paint

1. Cut a piece of string long enough to pass across your top lip and loop round each ear. Tie a loop at each end to fit round each ear.

1.

2. Cut a second, smaller piece of string which will loop from the first piece round your bottom lip. Tie this string to the first piece.

2.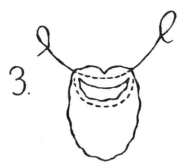

3. Glue the cotton wool or crêpe hair to the strings to make a beard and moustache.

3.

4. If you use cotton wool and do not want white facial hair, paint it the colour you require.

PUZZLE: QUICK QUIZ

Check how much information you have taken in so far by seeing if you can answer these questions.

1. How can you make yourself look smaller?
2. How can you make yourself walk with a genuine limp?
3. What feature is a real giveaway if you are trying to disguise yourself as a member of the opposite sex?
4. How can you make yourself speak with a lisp?
5. How can you make your skin darker without using make-up?
6. How can you make yourself look older?

HOW TO TAIL A SUSPECT

To 'tail' someone means to follow them without their knowledge. The best way to do this is to disguise yourself, so that if your suspect does spot you, he or she will not recognize you. You can follow any of the advice in the previous chapter to make yourself look different, but you could also adopt a whole disguise so you can act out a part. If, however, you have to change your appearance in a hurry in order to tail someone, put on a coat, hat and a pair of sunglasses and carry a newspaper. That way, if your suspect looks round, you can lurk in a doorway with your face hidden by the paper, peeping round the edge of it to see if the coast is clear. If you do not have a newspaper, pull out your mobile phone and lurk in a doorway, pretending to be listening to someone on the other end. But all the time you will, of course, be keeping an eye on your suspect.

While you are following your suspect, be on the lookout all the time for places you can dodge into and hide, such as doorways, garden gates, shop entrances and so on.

follow without being spotted

Acting a part

If you are tailing someone, or keeping a watch on their premises, it is a good idea to dress as if you are acting a part. You can then blend into the background and no one will notice you.

1. If you are lucky enough to have a small, portable tape recorder you can pretend to be a journalist or a market researcher and tape conversations without attracting attention.

2. If you wear an overall or dungarees and carry a bucket of water, a cloth and a squeegee you can pass as a window cleaner or a car windscreen cleaner.

3. If you or a friend have a newspaper round, use the bag as a prop, with a few papers sticking out

of it, and pretend to be delivering them.

4. If you own, or can borrow, a tracksuit, tie a band round your head, put on your trainers or plimsolls, and pretend to be a jogger.

5. Borrow a very old coat and hat, tie a piece of string round your middle, and pretend to be a tramp snoozing on a park bench or in a doorway.

6. Borrow some gardening tools (ask first!), wear an overall and pretend to be clipping a hedge or weeding a flower bed.

7. Carry some large carrier bags, or a holdall, and call at the house you are wanting to investigate pretending to collect old clothes and other bits and pieces for a jumble sale.

8. If you can borrow a pair of binoculars, you could pretend to be a birdwatcher. Complete the disguise with a book on birds and a notebook and pencil. This is a good disguise if you have to follow someone in a park or in the country because it gives you a reason for using binoculars without arousing anyone's suspicion.

PUZZLE: HOW MANY SPIES?

How many spies can you spot tailing the man in the stripy scarf in this picture?

PLACES FROM WHICH TO SPY

OUT OF DOORS

Telephone kiosk

Make sure you have plenty of loose change so you can pretend to be making a number of phone calls. Also carry a pencil and a notebook, so you can be seen jotting down information from your calls. You can also note down your observations! If the kiosk is in a busy place, you may have to let other people enter it every so often to make their own calls, or they could get very angry with you!

Behind a parked car

Crouching behind a car may be a good hiding-place for a short while, but you can get very uncomfortable if you stay there too long! Also, if you are on the pavement beside the car, hidden from your suspect, you will not be hidden on the pavement side and may attract some curious looks from passers-by.

Behind a tree

A large tree makes a good hiding-place. Again, people passing on the side where you are not hidden may be suspicious of you, but you could always pull out your newspaper and lean against the tree as though reading it while you are waiting for someone.

Up a tree

If the tree is not too small you may be able to climb it and hide in the branches. This will give you a very good view of what is happening beneath the tree, and you will also be able to hear what people are saying. You must be very careful when climbing trees. Don't go up too high, and never crawl along branches that may not support your weight. A good agent never takes unnecessary risks.

Behind a wall or fence

This is a good place from which to spy if your

suspect is just the other side of it, but if he or she moves away then you may have to make a long detour in order to catch up with them again and you could lose them.

In a dustbin

A really dedicated agent might consider hiding in a dustbin! If you can, wear rubber boots, gloves and overalls so you can discard them and wash them afterwards. Although unpleasant, a dustbin is quite a good hiding-place because you can peep out from under the lid to see what is going on. And no one will suspect you of hiding there!

INDOORS

If you know beforehand (and it's your job to find out!) where a meeting you wish to spy on is going to take place, then you can hide yourself in the room before it starts. Remember to go to the loo before you hide, so you don't get desperate, and take a handkerchief so you can press it against your nose if you feel you are going to sneeze. That would really give the game away!

Behind or under the furniture

You may be able to hide behind a sofa or a large chair, under a sideboard or table (if it has a long cloth on it this makes an excellent hiding-place), or even under a bed. Try to get comfortable before the meeting starts, so you don't fidget.

In a cupboard or wardrobe

If the cupboard or wardrobe is large enough this makes a very good hiding-place. You may be able to hide right behind the hanging clothes, so that even if someone looked in they would not see you. Leave the door open a little way, so you can breathe, and also so you can hear what is being said.

Behind the curtains

Full-length curtains also provide good cover when you want to hide. Make sure your feet are covered and not sticking out. If the curtains are only window-sill length, you can still hide behind them if the sill is wide enough for you to curl up on.

Behind a door

As long as no one is going to close the door you could hide behind it. Behind a door is a good place to hide if you have to conceal yourself quickly. You must be sure to leave the room before the others do, or flatten yourself back against the wall when they open the door and wait until they have all left before you move.

COPING WITH UNEXPECTED PROBLEMS

Escaping from a locked room

If someone locks you in a room and leaves the key in the door, there's an easy way to get out, assuming there's a slight gap under the door. Simply slide a sheet of paper under the door, leaving enough to get hold of on your side, then wiggle a pen, pencil or piece of wire in the keyhole on your side. This will dislodge the key, which will fall with a 'plop' on the sheet of paper you have pushed under the door. All you need to do then is slide the paper carefully back again, and the key will come with it. You can then unlock the door on your side and escape.

If the key has not been left in the door, but there is a window which will open and you are not on the ground floor, take down the curtains, or, if you are in a bedroom, take the sheets off the bed. Knot the curtains or sheets together to form a long 'rope'. Attach one end of the 'rope' to a heavy piece of furniture, making sure your knots are very firm. Put the rest of the 'rope' through the window. You can now climb carefully down it to the ground, walking down the wall with your feet and holding the 'rope' firmly between your hands. Do not use this method if you are higher up than the first floor! You may injure yourself, and then you will not be able to carry out your espionage duties.

Listening to a conversation in an adjoining room

If you do not have time to place hidden microphones in the room, hold the rim of a glass against the wall and put your ear to the bottom of the glass. It will magnify the sound coming from the adjoining room. If you cannot hear very well, move the glass around until you can. Depending on the structure of the wall, you will hear better in some places than others. Internal walls are usually made of a wooden framework and plasterboard, and the board will transmit the sound better than the wood.

Finding your way

If you are dumped by the enemy in the middle of a desert, a forest, or open moorland, and have to find your way home, here are two ways of making an instant compass.

The first is to use your watch, which you can do if the weather is sunny. Put your watch on the ground with the little hand pointing towards the sun. The point halfway between the 12 on your watch and the little hand will then be south. For example, if it is six o'clock, the 3 on your watch will be facing south.

The second method can be used at night or

on cloudy days. You will need to carry with you a needle and a length of thread, which you can pin carefully to the back of a coat lapel or inside a pocket. Before you leave home, magnetize the needle by stroking it gently with a magnet from the point to the eye. Do this several times. When you need to use the needle, tie the thread round the centre of it and hold it so it can spin round freely. When it has stopped spinning, the eye of the needle will point north.

PUZZLE: HIDING-PLACES

The words below are places you might use to spy from, but their letters have been jumbled up. Can you unscramble them?

NOLEETHEP SOKKI

DROPUBAC

RICTSNAU

TIDSUNB

BLEAT

BROWREAD

HOW TO CREATE SECRET CODES AND CIPHERS

Do you know the difference between a code and a cipher? Most of the systems we call codes, such as Morse code, are really ciphers. A cipher is a system in which every letter in the alphabet is replaced by another letter, number or symbol; a code is a system in which a whole sentence can be replaced by a single word, phrase, letter, number or symbol. A coded message is therefore shorter than the original text, so a code can be simple to remember, but a more complicated code needs a code book so both the writer and the receiver of the message can work out what it says. It's a bit like using a phrase book in a foreign country. This poses a danger, because a code book can easily fall into enemy hands. Here are some examples of code words you might use, and the messages you might use them for.

Code word	Message it conveys
Bulldog	Enemy agent arriving Wednesday.
Bloodhound	Tail the agent and report back.
Barker	Contact headquarters immediately.
Digger	Destroy your documents now.
Party	Meet your contact as arranged.
Sunglasses	Only go out in disguise.
Pack animals	I need help – send more agents.
Retriever	Pick up the report at the dead letter box.
Blind date	Meet me in the usual place at the usual time.
Amusement	I must see you urgently – contact me.

A different code system

You can avoid the danger of writing down your secrets and risking them falling into the hands of the enemy by using a different kind of code book. All you need are two identical copies of the same book, that is, not only the same title, but the same edition. You keep one, your contact has the other. It doesn't matter what book you use. It could be a favourite novel, a school textbook or even a dictionary. You use it by finding the words of the message you want to pass on in different pages of the book. Then you write down the places where you found them. For example, the first word might appear on page 6, line 13 (counting down from the top of the page), and be the fifth word along the line. So the code for the word would be 6: 13: 5. Working out the message in this way will leave you with a row of numbers in groups of three – a code which is uncrackable by anyone who does not know which book you are using to create it. It is, therefore, a very safe code to use.

CIPHERS

Morse code is probably the best known cipher. It is a system of dots and dashes, which can be represented by flashes of light, tapping, or graph-like zig-zags. Here are the basic code,

A ·—	H ····	O ———	V ···—
B —···	I ··	P ·——·	W ·——
C —·—·	J ·———	Q ——·—	X —··—
D —··	K —·—	R ·—·	Y —·——
E ·	L ·—··	S ···	Z ——··
F ··—·	M ——	T —	
G ——·	N —·	U ··—	

and the zig-zag version of it.

A ⋀   H ⋀⋀⋀   O ⋀⋀⋀   V ⋀⋀⋀
B ⋀⋀   I ⋀   P ⋀⋀   W ⋀⋀
C ⋀⋀⋀   J ⋀⋀⋀   Q ⋀⋀⋀   X ⋀⋀⋀
D ⋀⋀   K ⋀⋀   R ⋀⋀   Y ⋀⋀⋀
E ⋀   L ⋀⋀⋀   S ⋀⋀   Z ⋀⋀⋀
F ⋀⋀⋀   M ⋀⋀   T ⋀
G ⋀⋀⋀   N ⋀⋀   U ⋀⋀

Can you work out what this message says?

⋀⋀ ⋀ ⋀⋀ ⋀⋀ ⋀ ⋀⋀

⋀ ⋀

⋀ ⋀⋀ ⋀⋀ ⋀ ⋀⋀ ⋀⋀ ⋀⋀⋀

⋀⋀ ⋀ ⋀⋀⋀

⋀⋀ ⋀

⋀⋀ ⋀⋀⋀ ⋀ ⋀⋀ ⋀⋀ ⋀ ⋀ ⋀⋀

⋀⋀ ⋀ ⋀⋀ ⋀ ⋀⋀ ⋀

Semaphore

Semaphore is a signalling system using flags held in different positions to represent different letters.

What message do these flags spell out?

Substitution ciphers

These can be as simple or as complicated as you like. One of the simplest is A = 1, B = 2, and so on. But you could reverse it, and have A = 26, B = 25, and so on. Or you could be sneaky and have A = D, B = E. All these versions appear below, so you can use them to send your own messages.

A = 1	A = 26	A = D
B = 2	B = 25	B = E
C = 3	C = 24	C = F
D = 4	D = 23	D = G
E = 5	E = 22	E = H
F = 6	F = 21	F = I
G = 7	G = 20	G = J
H = 8	H = 19	H = K
I = 9	I = 18	I = L
J = 10	J = 17	J = M
K = 11	K = 16	K = N
L = 12	L = 15	L = O
M = 13	M = 14	M = P
N = 14	N = 13	N = Q
O = 15	O = 12	O = R
P = 16	P = 11	P = S
Q = 17	Q = 10	Q = T
R = 18	R = 9	R = U
S = 19	S = 8	S = V

T = 20	T = 7	T = W
U = 21	U = 6	U = X
V = 22	V = 5	V = Y
W = 23	W = 4	W = Z
X = 24	X = 3	X = A
Y = 25	Y = 2	Y = B
Z = 26	Z = 1	Z = C

Using these ciphers, can you read the following messages?

a) 3 15 12 12 5 3 20   16 1 18 3 5 12   1 20
   19 20 1 20 9 15 14

b) 14 22 22 7   14 22   7 6 22 8 23 26 2   18 13
   24 26 21 22

c) W K L Q N   W K H B   D U H   R Q
   W R   P H   V H Q G   K H O S

The messages have been written out in blocks of numbers or letters which correspond to the letters in the real word. But if you wanted to be really sneaky, you could divide them up differently. So message no. 1 could look like this, for example:

3 15 12   12 5 3 20 16 1 18   3 5 12 1 20
19 20 1 20   9 15 14.

42

Did you notice anything about the frequency with which certain letters or numbers crop up? It may help you to know, when you have to decode other messages, that the letter most frequently used in the English language is E. So the letter or number that appears most often in the coded message is likely to be E. (See page 61 for more information about the frequency of letters used in English.)

Misleading division

As we saw above, you can divide up messages in the wrong places to deliberately confuse people. For example, can you read this message?

ENE MYFLY INGTOP ARI SIW ILLFO LLOW

Phoney firsts

Another simple way of confusing your enemies is to add a phoney false letter to the beginning of every word. The message above, written out with phoney first letters, might read:

WENEMY PFLYING STO IPARIS MI TWILL EFOLLOW.

Phoney lasts

You can also add a phoney last letter to each word.

Here's another message using phoney lasts. Can you read it?

SUSPECTH MK OFT BEINGY SPYL KEEPG CLOSEW WATCHT ONG HIME.

Phoney lasts double bluff

To make this a bit more complicated, use a phoney last letter in place of the real last letter, and put the real last letter in front of the next word in the message.

SUSPECX TML OT FBEINJ GSPK YKEER PCLOSR EWATCB HOP NHIMK.

Back to front

You can either write the whole message back to front from the beginning, or you can write each word in the message back to front.

WOLLOF OT TXET TENRETNI FFO EGASSEM PU DEKCIP

DEKCIP PU EGASSEM FFO TENRETNI TXET OT WOLLOF

Null cipher

A null is a meaningless letter, and you can put one either in front of each of the real letters in the message, after each letter, or both in front and after each letter. It is a simple cipher, but it makes the real words look wonderfully double Dutch. Here are examples of each of the ways of using nulls described above. Can you read them?

1. S M J U L S E T   T M B A D K P E
   N C D O L N A T L A Y C W T
   N W D I K T O H   L G K E D O S
   R B G D E   E S A E D N B D
   G A B D E D T R L E T S W S

2. M D U N S P T X   M V A P K H E J
   C L O G N E T S A W C N T M
   W B I J T L H N   G D E R O P R S
   G D E M   S Y E I N Q D M
   A W D B D L R T E B S P S D

3. E M D U P S K T M   G M D A B K P E R
   W C H O C N J T M A P C Q T Y
   V W Y I U T L H J
   P G Q E B O N R M G H E L
   P S D E P N W D K
   B A R D L D G R T E P S W S T

Column cipher

Take a message like this:

SENDING   YOU   MICROFILM   IN
CHRISTMAS CAKE.

If you write it out in two columns, like this:

S	L
E	M
N	I
D	N
I	C
N	H
G	R
Y	I
O	S
U	T
M	M
I	A
C	S
R	C
O	A
F	K
I	E

Then read across and divide it into groups of

letters, like this:

S L E M N I   D N I C   N H G R Y I
O S U T   M M I A   C S R C O A
F K I E

It looks very different, doesn't it? But if you know it is a column cipher, you will find it quite easy to decode.

Rail-fence cipher

This is another simple cipher which is very effective. You write your message on two lines, putting every other letter on the lower line. For example, if your message is:

ENEMY MASTER SPY ARRIVING FROM AFRICA

you write it like this:

E E Y A T R   P   A R V N   F O   A R C
 N M M S E   S Y   R I I G   R M   F I A

Then you write out the top line followed by the bottom line, dividing the letters up into random groups, like this:

E E Y A T R P A R V N F O
A R C. N M M S E S Y R I I G
R M F I A

You may notice there is a dot halfway through it –
this is to show the end of the first line.

Rosicrucian/Pigpen cipher

This is based on a cipher invented in the 16th
century by a man from Naples called Giovanni
Porta. You draw four figures as shown below, and
then fill them with letters. Each symbol then stands
for a single letter.

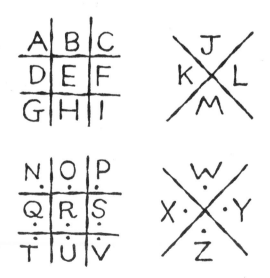

Can you work out what the following message says?

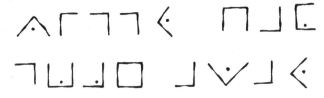

Box cipher

If you make a grid of, say, 36 squares, and write your message in it, it will look incomprehensible to someone who doesn't know which way to read the message. But it will make perfect sense to someone who does. Look at this example.

L	U	P	R	T	M
E	R	U	A	G	E
C	G	K	I	N	E
R	E	C	N	I	T
A	N	I	T	N	M
P	T	P	O	R	O

You might pick out the word URGENT, but otherwise the letters don't seem to make much sense, do they? Try reading them down one column and then up the next, starting at the top right-hand corner, and you'll discover what the message says.

Code grille

Take an ordinary-looking letter, like this.

Dear Amy,

How are you? It seems a long time since we met. I hope you haven't caught a cold or flu this winter.

Dad is complaining of molehills on the lawn, yet does nothing about them. But Mum and I like the creatures. On the subject of animals, did you see John and his dog on TV tracking rabbits? More news on this when we meet.

Come and see us soon.

Love,
Brenda.

It looks quite innocent, doesn't it? But put a piece of paper with boxes cut out of it over the letter – and see what you can read. In order to use a code grille both you and the person you are sending the message to need a copy of the grille so you know where in the letter to put the words that form the message. Once you have done that, you can use it as many times as you like.

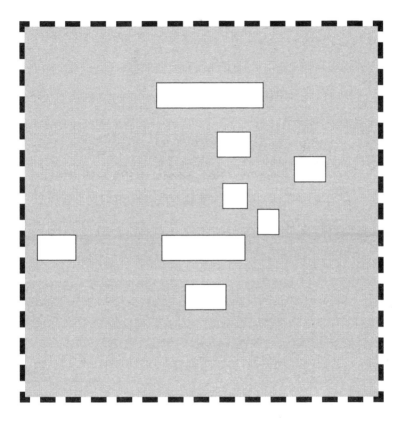

Pinhole code

In a similar way, you can write an apparently ordinary letter and stick a pin under the words of the message you want to send. It might look something like this. (Because we cannot print a book with holes in the pages we have represented them by dots.)

Dear Bill,

I hope to see you on Saturday to help you mend your bike. I've lost my puncture repair outfit, and its instructions – could you please get me another?

Anne asked me to send her love to Carol. She told me she will bring a copy of her favourite comic when she calls next week.

Love,
Ben.

Can you read the message?

Trevanion's cipher

Sir John Trevanion was a cavalier who was caught and imprisoned in Colchester Castle during the English Civil War. A number of his friends who had also been caught had been executed, and Sir John faced the same fate.

He was allowed to receive letters, and one day

his gaoler handed him this one, having previously scanned it and decided it was perfectly innocent. The language is that of the 17th century.

Worthie Sir John: Hope, that is the beste comfort of the afflicted, cannot much, I fear me, help you now. That I would saye to you, is this only: if ever I may be able to requite that I do owe you, stand not upon asking me. 'Tis not much I can do: but what I can do, bee you verie sure I wille. I knowe that, if dethe comes, if ordinary men fear it, it frights not you, accounting it for a high honour, to have such a rewarde of your loyalty. Pray yet that you may be spared this soe bitter, cup. I fear not that you will grudge any sufferings; onlie if bie submission you can turn them away, 'tis the part of a wise man. Tell me, as if you can, to do for you any thinge that you wolde have done. The general goes back on Wednesday. Restinge your servant to command.

R.T.

Having read his letter, Sir John asked if he might be taken to the prison chapel to pray and meditate. The guard agreed. The chapel had only one door and its windows were small, narrow and set high up in the walls. It appeared to be escape-proof. But when the guard realized that Sir John had been in the chapel rather a long time, he decided to investigate, and found the room empty. It was a great mystery – his prisoner seemed to have vanished into thin air. But had he known the message concealed in the letter Sir John had received, he would not have been so surprised. If you read every third letter after each punctuation mark, it spells out the message:

PANEL AT EAST END OF CHAPEL SLIDES.

And that is how the prisoner escaped.

You can, of course, construct a cipher of your own based on punctuation. Suppose you take the letter that comes immediately after each punctuation mark in the following message. What does it spell out?

Colin told me, 'Fred is your man, only don't let him, laddie, lie to you about his family. Otherwise he will be a helpful, willing worker, sure to be there when you need him, unusually neat and tidy, swift to see what is needed. Peter may also come and help you pick the fruit. Even if he's busy he may find an hour or two. Clive is away, taking his mother to London.'

Code wheel

To make a code wheel, you must draw and cut out two discs of paper or card and mark them with letters of the alphabet.

You will need
Paper or card
A pair of compasses
Pen or pencil
Scissors
Paper fastener

1. Draw two circles on the paper or card, one about 2 cm smaller in diameter than the other. Cut them out.
2. Round the edge of the larger circle, write the letters of the alphabet in a clockwise direction. If you also want to have a number cipher, add numbers from 1 to 26.
3. Round the edge of the smaller circle, write the letters of the alphabet in an anti-clockwise direction. Add an arrow beside the A.
4. Put the smaller disc on top of the larger, and join them together in the centre with a paper fastener.
5. You can now turn the smaller disc independently of the larger one.

6. To send a message, decide on a letter. Let us say it is S.

7. Turn the A of the smaller circle to point to the S on the larger one and keep the wheels in this position.

8. Now, using the letters of the smaller circle as those of the real message, and those of the outer circle as those of the encoded message, how would you send the following message in code?

FRASER ARRIVING HEATHROW
MONDAY.

Text messaging and emails

These are ideal ways of sending messages in code. With some pay phones you can even send an anonymous text message. You can simply abbreviate your message, e.g.:

SEE YOU TOMORROW,
WAIT AT BUS STOP

can be abbreviated to:

CU2MORO, W8 AT BS.

But this is a bit too easy for someone else to read! So, using your knowledge of ciphers, turn your normal text message into a coded text message. For example, using the simple substitution cipher on page 41, in which A=1, B=2, and so on, your text message would end up like this:

3 21 B 13 15 18 15 23 H 1 20 2 19.

Note that the digits in the text message have been turned back into letters. Sneaky, isn't it? Can you work out what this one means?

4 9 4 21 3 14 5 A 6 12 12 23 7 21

You can use email in this way as well, and can have as many different email addresses as you need.

Body language

'Body language' means the small movements we make, such as scratching our heads, rubbing our noses, and so on. These can be used to pass messages to a contact without using any words at all, and without anyone suspecting that a message is even being transmitted. You need to agree a code between your contact and yourself. It could be something like this:

Movement   **Message**

Scratching your head   You are being watched, take care

Rubbing your nose   Yes

Blowing your nose   No

Pulling your ear	Follow that person (a meaningful look will indicate which one)
Rubbing your eye	You are in danger, leave now
Sitting down	Relax, he/she is not the enemy
Sitting down and crossing your legs	Be careful what you say

Rubbing your chin with one finger	Take great care, he/she is the enemy
Folding your arms and leaving a certain number of fingers showing	This is a way of expressing numbers

You can, of course, invent your own system of body language and messages.

invent your own language

Colour and clothing codes

With a pre-arranged system, the wearing of certain types of clothing, or particular colours, can pass on a message. For example, wearing a jacket might mean, 'All is well'; wearing a jumper might mean, 'I'm following a suspect'. Wearing a hat might mean 'yes', not wearing one could mean 'no'. If you're a girl, you could pass on a different message according to whether you are wearing a skirt or trousers.

With the colour code, you need not necessarily wear a shirt or trousers in the particular colour. A scarf, a handkerchief sticking out of a pocket, a belt or a badge would do. Red is traditionally the colour for danger, green for all clear, so it might be as well to decide on different meanings for these colours. You could, for example, create a code like this:

Colour	Meaning
Red	You're quite safe
White	Danger, look out
Green	You're being followed
Blue	Arrange a meeting with X as soon as possible

Black	Contact headquarters
Purple	Check the suspect's room
Pink	All the agents must meet at the usual place
Yellow	Change your disguise, they're on to you

CODE-BREAKING

If an enemy's code messages fall into your hands you can use your knowledge of codes and ciphers to try to decode them. First of all check if you can simply divide up the groups of letters differently to make words. If you cannot, or if you are facing a page full of numbers or symbols, you have to tackle a substitution cipher. If this is the case, check which numbers or symbols occur most frequently. As we have seen, E is the letter used most often in the English language. After E, the frequency with which letters occur in English is as follows:

T A O N R I S H D L F C M U G Y P W B V K X J Q Z.

So if a message contains a lot of Bs, Vs, Xs and Qs it is likely to be a substitution cipher.

PUZZLE: CODE MESSAGES

All the words listed below connected with codes, ciphers and sending messages are hidden in the grid opposite. Can you find them all? The words may read across, up, down or diagonally, either forwards or backwards, but they are all in straight lines. The letters may be used in more than one word, but not all of the letters are necessarily used.

ANONYMOUS

CIPHER

COMMUNICATION

CONFIDENTIAL

CODE

CODE-BREAKING

CRYPTOGRAM

ENIGMA

MEMO

MESSAGE

MORSE

NEWS

NULL

PARCEL

SEMAPHORE

SEND

SIGNAL

SYMBOL

SUBSTITUTION

TOP SECRET
(2 lines)

WRITING

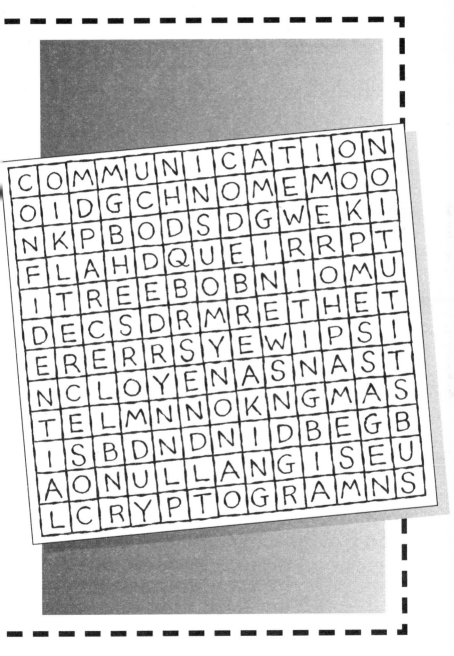

C	O	M	M	U	N	I	C	A	T	I	O	N
O	I	D	G	C	H	N	O	M	E	M	O	O
N	K	P	B	O	D	S	D	G	W	E	K	I
F	L	A	H	D	Q	U	E	I	R	R	P	T
I	T	R	E	E	B	O	B	N	I	O	M	U
D	E	C	S	D	R	M	R	E	T	H	E	T
E	R	E	R	R	S	Y	E	W	I	P	S	I
N	C	L	O	Y	E	N	A	S	N	A	S	T
T	E	L	M	N	N	O	K	N	G	M	A	S
I	S	B	D	N	D	N	I	D	B	E	G	B
A	O	N	U	L	L	A	N	G	I	S	E	U
L	C	R	Y	P	T	O	G	R	A	M	S	

63

PASSING SECRET MESSAGES TO YOUR CONTACT

In these days of emails and text messages passing secret messages to your contact appears to be simple, but you cannot always use electronic devices. If your enemy is clever enough, he or she may intercept them, and simply being seen using a mobile phone can arouse suspicion. So it is as well to have a knowledge of some of the traditional ways in which agents have passed on information. But make sure you only leave a message in a public place such as those described below if you are sure that your contact will be along very soon to collect it.

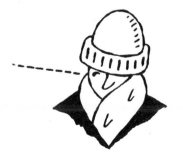

Dead letter boxes

A dead letter box is a place where you hide a message for your contact to pick up later. A classic hiding-place is in the bark of a hollow tree, and you could use this if there is a suitable tree in a park both you and your contact visit. Wherever you leave your message, you must take care that it cannot be seen by a casual passer-by.

In a park or garden

Apart from inside a tree, you can hide a message under a stone, in a crack between two bricks or stones in a wall, and even buried in the earth. Wrap the message carefully in a waterproof cover and hide it just beneath the earth under or next to a special plant or shrub. Or put it under a stone or a paving slab.

You could also tape a message to the underside of a park bench, a swing, a roundabout, a slide or another piece of playground equipment. Or hide it under an overhanging part of a statue. With a false message stuck over the top, you could pin it up on a noticeboard. If you know your contact will be along very shortly, you could hide the message in a chocolate-bar wrapper and throw it into a litter bin.

At a bus stop

You can push the message behind the timetable, if there is one; tape it to the underneath of a seat in a bus shelter, or fold it up small and stick it to the back of a used bus ticket and put it in the litter bin.

In a café

If you go into the café before your contact you can leave your message under the sugar bowl, or the salt (or pepper, or tomato sauce, or whatever is left on the table). Or you could slide it under the tablecloth and leave it for your contact to pick up later.

At your contact's house

If you wear the right disguise, you could actually deliver the message to your contact's house. Pretend to be a postman, and put the message through the letter box with some old envelopes which look like the post. Dress like a milkman, and leave the message in an empty milk bottle, or disguise yourself as the paper boy or girl and hide the message in a newspaper and put it through the letter box. You could even be a window cleaner and leave a message stuck to the underneath of a window ledge.

In the cinema

You have to pre-arrange this, but you agree a seat row and number with your contact first. You go to the earlier showing of the film and leave the message taped to the underneath of the seat or the armrest. Then your contact goes to the later showing of the film, to the same seat, and retrieves the message.

On the beach

Wrap the message in a waterproof bag and bury it in the sand by a rock or under a sandcastle. But make sure that your burial place is above the high-water mark, or the tide will sweep away the message. If you are going to meet your contact on the beach (there is more about passing  messages directly to your contacts a few pages on) and you want to be really daring, wrap your message in a waterproof bag, buy an ice-cream cornet and poke the wrapped message down into the ice cream. Pass it to your contact, who should be just behind you in the queue, as if you have just bought it for him or her. No one watching will ever suspect how important that ice cream is!

In the gym

Tape the message to the underneath of a piece of equipment such as a vaulting horse or trampoline. Or hide it under a mat, tape it to a rope, to weights, or behind the wall bars. There are a great many places to hide a message in a gym. You will have to choose a place that is convenient both for your contact and yourself.

In the library

Hand in a library book with the message written on a piece of paper slipped between two of its pages. When you leave the library, your contact enters and asks for the same book. Choose a title that is not too popular, otherwise another borrower might snatch it up before your contact can do so.

MAKING PERSONAL CONTACT

Sometimes it is not safe to leave a message unattended and you have to meet your contact to pass it on.

In the café

If you meet your contact in the café you must pretend not to know him or her. The contact can come up to you and ask if a seat at your table is free. You of course say 'yes', but otherwise you do not talk to your companion. Then he or she could ask you to pass the sugar, which you do, having previously hidden the message in it. Or you could drop a napkin with the message wrapped in it and your contact could pick it up for you and take out the message before handing it back to you.

In the street

When you meet your contact in the street it must seem like an accidental encounter. So, for example, you could both be carrying identical umbrellas, parcels or shopping bags. You pretend to bump into each other, both drop whatever you were carrying, then, as you scuffle to pick it up, you each pick up the other's property.

Or you could hide your message in a piece of waste paper and toss it into a bin. Your contact is following you and retrieves it instantly. He or she could pretend to be a tramp and poke around in the bin before pocketing the message.

In the park

Sit casually reading a newspaper on a park bench. After a while, get up and stroll away, leaving the paper on the bench for your contact to pick up. The message is, of course, hidden in the paper.

If you have a dog, take it for a walk in the park with the message attached to its collar. Meet your contact as if bumping into a stranger. He or she bends down to pat the dog and while doing so removes the message from its collar.

If you want to be really clever, write your message on a scarf in such a way that it appears to be part of the design. Put the scarf loosely in your pocket and allow it to fall out, as if accidentally. Your contact can then come along and pick it up. Make sure no one else is around to find it first, though!

On a bus or train

You and your contact both catch the same bus or train but sit separately. You tuck the message down the side or back of the seat, then stand up in order to get off the bus or train. Your contact goes to sit in your seat and retrieves the message.

At a party or disco

This is a good place to pass on a message as it is likely to be dimly lit and crowded. Dance near your contact and you will find it quite easy to pass the message to him or her.

At football practice

Stick the message on to the ball and kick it to your contact, who should pretend to be practising his goalkeeping skills. He can easily remove the message and tuck it up his sleeve or in his pocket while retrieving the ball.

This method can also be used with other ball games.

At the swimming pool

If you can swim underwater, this can be an excellent place to pass on a message, as absolutely no one will suspect you! Put the message in a waterproof wrapping or write it with indelible ink on greaseproof paper. Tuck it into your swimsuit and pretend to bump into your contact underwater. As you do so, pass the message on to him or her.

PUZZLE: HOW MANY MESSAGES?

Here's a test of your powers of observation. Study these two pictures carefully. How many

secret messages can you spot hidden in each picture? And how many differences are there between the pictures?

HOW TO MAKE AND USE INVISIBLE INK

To make doubly sure of your message being safe from enemy eyes, you could write it in invisible ink. No, you cannot buy invisible ink in an invisible bottle at a stationer's – but it is very easy to make. The following substances, which you will find in the average house, all make good invisible inks.

Lemonade, or other fizzy drinks
A sugar solution – made by adding a teaspoonful of sugar to a glass of water and dissolving it
Orange, lemon or grapefruit juice
Apple juice
Onion juice – scrape the onion with your 'pen' – see below

Potato juice – use as onion juice
Honey dissolved in warm water – use a teaspoonful to a glass of water
Vinegar, use undiluted
Milk, preferably skimmed or semi-skimmed. The cream, being fatty, will leave a stain
Salt – a teaspoonful dissolved in a glass of water
Bicarbonate of soda – a teaspoonful dissolved in a glass of water

Whatever substance you use, you will need a 'pen' to write with. You might use a matchstick (wooden end only), or the clip on the top of a cheap plastic ballpoint pen. You can use a number of different things – the only criterion being that they must not make a mark on the paper, or your message will not be invisible. Dip the 'pen' in the ink and write your message on the paper. Because you cannot see what you are writing it is as well to work it out beforehand, especially if it is in code, and write it out with a pen or pencil and then copy it out in your invisible ink. Of course, you must destroy the paper on which you worked it out.

When your contact receives your message, he or she must develop it, like a photograph, in order to read it. This is a very simple process – all you need is a source of heat. Hold the paper over a radiator and, hey presto, the writing will magically appear! It will be a brownish colour, and once it has been developed, it will stay visible so your contact will have to destroy it. If you do not have a hot radiator you can use, then hold the paper near a light bulb. *Never* risk holding it near an open fire – the message may go up in flames and you may get hurt. A good agent is far too valuable to be put at risk in this way. Sending an apparently blank sheet of paper to your contact will arouse suspicion if it does fall into enemy hands, so it is a good idea to write a perfectly ordinary and innocent message on one side of the paper, with the invisible message on the back.

More invisible writing

Another way of producing an invisible message is to write it with a candle. You can use a narrow candle, such as people put on birthday cakes, or a piece of an ordinary-sized candle. Write your message on a smooth, uncreased piece of paper. When you have written the message it will be invisible. To read it, sprinkle talcum powder on the paper then shake or blow it off. The powder will stick to the candle wax, but not to the paper, enabling you to read the message. You can also rub a coloured wax crayon over the paper to reveal the message. It will stick to the plain paper, but not to the message written in wax.

Copying secret documents

If you need to copy a document and you have neither your special miniature camera with you, nor access to a photocopier, you need a bottle of special copying solution, which you can easily make at home. To make it, very carefully mix together a teaspoonful of turpentine, a teaspoonful of washing-up liquid, and two teaspoonfuls of water in a clean bottle with a screw cap. A small drinks bottle, well washed out, would work well. To copy a document, either brush the solution over it, or apply it with a sponge or a damp cloth. When you have done this, put a sheet of clean white paper down on top of the document and press it down firmly. When you lift off the paper, you will find the document printed in reverse on it. All you need do then is hold the paper in front of a mirror to read the writing.

PUZZLE: HIDDEN SUBSTANCES

Each of the sentences below conceals one or more names of some of the substances that can be used to make invisible ink. Can you spot them all?

1. Each one yelled out a name.
2. Would you plant a vine, Gary, in your garden?
3. I'm asking Dale, Mona Denton and Sal to my party.
4. Emil, Ken and Harry brought sandwiches.
5. Put your books together in a heap, please.
6. Then add to the pot a tomato.

HIDING SECRET PAPERS AND EQUIPMENT

IN YOUR ROOM

It is dangerous to leave your precious papers and equipment lying around in your room where an enemy agent may find them. With a bit of ingenuity you can create some very effective hiding-places.

Hiding papers

Slim items like papers are the easiest to hide. You can tape them to the underneath of various items of furniture such as tables and chairs. If you take a drawer out of a chest of drawers you can tape a document to the underneath of the drawer. Small items may also be hidden in the space behind the drawer, though make sure the drawer will still close, or it will attract attention and may reveal your hiding-place. You can also tape papers to the backs of pictures. If you can take the back off the picture and slip the document inside it, this makes an excellent hiding-place that is very unlikely to be discovered.

If you have an old book that is not too important to you or you anyone else, or you can buy a cheap one in a charity shop, tape two pages together along the base and up the sides to make a secret pocket in which you can hide a document. You could also use the pages of a magazine in the same way.

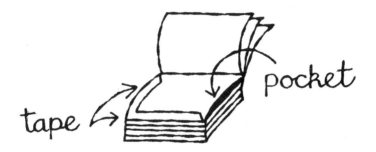

If you have to hide papers in a hurry you can slip them under your mattress, inside a pillowcase, or under the carpet or a mat on the floor.

If you have lined curtains you can hide a document between the curtain and the lining by pinning it to the lining.

A talcum-powder tin is a traditional hiding-place used by secret agents. Talcum powder comes in a variety of types of containers, and you need one which has a removable top. Take off the top, roll up your papers, secure them with an elastic band, pop them in the tin and replace the top. Put the talc back in the bathroom among the other bath things, or on your dressing-table, if you have one, so no one will notice it.

Hiding small objects

Rolls of film, cassettes, magnifying glasses and parts of your disguise also need to be kept in secret places.

Some small objects can be hidden in the toe of a sock, which can then be rolled up with its partner and hidden among the other socks in your drawer. If you have a clock with a removable back that, too, makes a good hiding-place.

A vase or ornamental jug is also useful. But you must put something in the vase or jug over your equipment to hide it. A bunch of dried flowers is good because people will think that is all the vase holds.

If you wrap the object in a polythene bag you could hide it in the earth of a potted plant, but take care that you don't leave a telltale scattering of compost around or it may put the enemy on the track.

If you have a thick book that no one wants any

more, or you can buy one cheaply at a charity shop (paperbacks often sell for a few pence), then you can make it into an excellent hiding place by gluing its pages together and then cutting a section out of the centre of them to form a box. Put your equipment inside, then hide the book on your bookshelves among your other books. It will not arouse the least bit of suspicion!

glue pages together

The classic hiding-place used by spies for generations is under a loose floorboard. If you happen to have one in your room, lift it up and hide your equipment in the space beneath it, then cover it with the carpet or mat. Don't go prising up boards that aren't loose, though, or you will be very unpopular with your parents!

IN YOUR CLOTHES

You can hide your secrets in your clothes when they are put away in your wardrobe or drawers. But clothes are also very useful for concealing messages and equipment when you want to take them somewhere.

Small items or folded messages can be pinned inside a tie, under a collar, under the folded-back cuffs of a jumper, in trouser turn-ups, in your socks or shoes, pinned to the lining of a hat or in the folds of a scarf or handkerchief. There are many choices. Use Blu-tack to stick a piece of paper to the inside of your belt, round the handle of your umbrella, or on the strap of your bag.

If you have time to prepare your clothing for carrying secret messages, you could make a false pocket lining to hide inside your own pocket. Fold over a piece of fabric and sew up both sides, to make a little bag. Then sew or pin it inside your real pocket. Put the secret message at the bottom of your real pocket, with the false pocket over the top of it, then fill the false pocket with all the things you would normally carry in it – a hanky, a coin or two, a pencil stub, some sweets, and so on. Leaving it empty would look suspicious – people almost never have empty pockets.

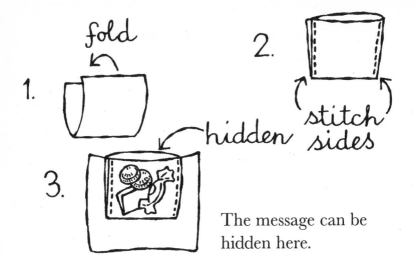

fold

1.

2.

stitch sides

3. hidden

The message can be hidden here.

Inside your shoes makes a good hiding-place. If you have some thin cardboard you can make the hiding-place even more secure by making false linings to your shoes. Stand each shoe on the cardboard and draw round it. Then cut out the card about one centimetre inside your drawing line, so that the false sole will fit inside your shoe. Make two so both shoes look the same, and hide your secret message under one of them.

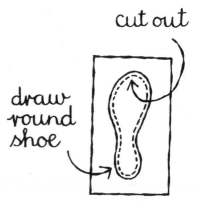

cut out

draw round shoe

Making the message part of your clothes

If you have the kind of coloured felt-tip pens that contain washable, not permanent, ink, you can write a message on a scarf, a tie, a handkerchief or even your socks. If you are clever, you can make your message look like part of the existing design. Or, even better, you could use clothes you have bought at a charity shop for this purpose, so you don't annoy your parents!

You can create badges by cutting out small discs of cardboard and taping safety pins to the back of them. On the badges create a design and hide a message in it. For instance, if you write your message very small and swirl it around the badge it will just look like a pattern. You could write a false message on it so no one will think of looking for the real one.

If you carry a pen that can be unscrewed into two halves, you can hide a small message inside it and carry the pen around with you as usual.

PUZZLE: WHO'S THE INTRUDER?

When you return to your room you discover someone has been in it. The hair that you stuck across the drawer where you keep your codebooks has gone, and there is another clue also. The intruder is likely to be one of these four people. Can you work out which one it is?

Colm   Rebecca   Nita

Sam

MAKING YOUR ROOM PROOF AGAINST ENEMY AGENTS

No matter how careful you are, if you are acting as a secret agent you are likely to have enemy agents on your trail trying to find out your secrets. It is important, therefore, to leave your room set up so you will know if anyone has been snooping around in it.

Leaving false information around

One way of hiding your secrets is to leave a trail of false information so that anyone snooping on you will think it is the real thing and not look any further. For example, make a false code book and leave it in a fairly prominent (but not too obvious) place, such as on your bookshelf, but not lying open on a table. (Hide your real code book under the mattress.)

Checking for intruders

Pull out one or two hairs from your head, lick your finger, moisten the hairs with it and stick them across a door or drawer in which you keep important things. The hairs will be virtually invisible, but if someone opens the door or drawer the hairs will fall off. If you look carefully you will see that they have gone and you will know that someone has been in your room.

Then you can dust for fingerprints. Shake a little talcum powder on any surface an intruder might have touched to reveal the prints. Stretch a piece of transparent sticky tape across them to lift them off and then stick the tape on to a sheet of dark paper so you can see them properly. You will need to compare them with your own, which will be all over your room, before you will know for sure if a stranger has left them. To do this, rub some hand cream on to your hands and then, with first one hand and then with the other, get hold of a clean, polished drinking glass. Wash your hands, then dust the glass with talc as described above, and lift the prints with tape and file them on dark paper for future reference. You will need to keep them to compare them with any other prints you find in order to detect which are the alien ones.

Leave a pile of papers on your table with a faint,

thin pencil line drawn down the side of the pile. If anyone handles the papers, the line will become jagged and you will know they have been there.

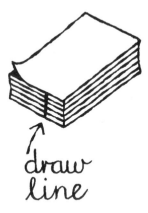

draw
line

If you leave a drawer very slightly open, make a faint pencil mark on its side to mark its position. If anyone opens the drawer to search through it they are very unlikely to be able to put back the drawer in exactly the same position.

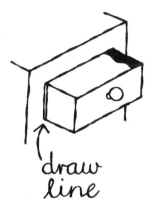

draw
line

Making a warning alarm

If you are some distance from your room and want an instant warning of someone entering it, or if you are in a highly secret meeting and want advance warning of someone approaching, you need to make an alarm.

You will need

Several empty drinks cans
Large paper clips
Black cotton
Drawing pins

1. Tie a length of black cotton to the centre of the long side of each paper clip. In the other end of the cotton tie a small loop. You will need as many paper clips as you have drinks cans.

2. Slip each paper clip inside the hole in the top of the can, holding it horizontally. You will now be able to suspend the can from the cotton.

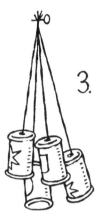

3. Slip the drawing pin through the loops on the ends of the cotton and pin the cans up on the inside of your door. If anyone opens the door they will make the most terrible noise!

To make an alarm to warn you of someone's approach, prepare the cans as before but tie them to a long piece of cotton. Pin it to the skirting boards across the corridor leading to your room, or some other suitable place, about 8 cm above the ground. Stretch the cotton taut as far as the cans, and tuck them away out of sight. When someone walks along they will trip over the cotton and the cans will clatter noisily as before.

PUZZLE: CHECK YOUR PRINTS

Use your sharp powers of observation to spot which two of these fingerprints are exactly the same.

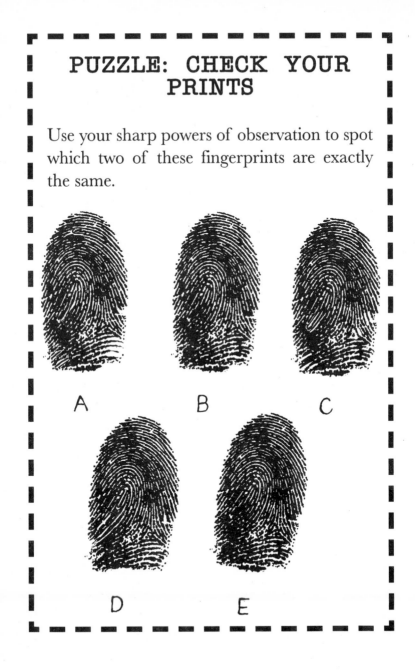

A

B

C

D

E

COUNTER-ESPIONAGE

This does not mean spying in a shop, it means spying on and, if possible, putting out of action, your enemies. You have to be on the lookout for agents spying on you at all times. Be suspicious of approaches by people who offer you information – he or she may be a double agent. One of the first things you must learn is to trust no one. Even someone you thought was a friend and fellow agent may have defected to the enemy and no longer be on your side, so never allow them access to your secret information.

Avoiding being bugged

If you enter a strange room, expect it to be bugged. Look for microphones behind pictures, in vases of flowers, in light fittings and on bookshelves. If you cannot find one, but think it may be present somewhere, take great care if you have to speak to your contact in that room. If there is a radio, turn it on to drown your voices. Better still, if there is a washbasin, turn on the tap and run the water. Running water 'scrambles' sound very effectively.

Losing a shadow

Always be aware that you may be being shadowed by the enemy. When you are walking down the street, look round every so often to see if someone is following you. If you see someone suddenly stop and bend down to tie their shoelace, be suspicious. Duck into a shop, preferably a large, crowded one, and try to lose them. Leave the shop by a different door. If someone follows you on to a bus or train, either get off at the next stop or go right to the terminus, to fool them. Do not follow the plan you had in mind or you may lead the enemy straight to your secrets.

Look carefully at people who come to your door. If the postman, the paper boy and the window-cleaner all look alike, you are being watched! Do not confront your shadow, but lead him or her on a false trail leading to wrong information. This will keep them busy for some time, giving you time to warn your contacts, and change your codes and meeting places.

A good spy can never relax. If you keep alert at all times, you will carry out your duties well and be a highly successful agent.

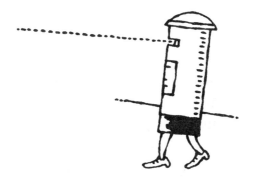

A SECRET AGENT'S GLOSSARY

When you are still learning to be a secret agent you may come across some words and phrases whose meaning you are unsure of. This glossary will help you to understand them.

Agent Another name for a spy; a person who acts on behalf of someone else.

Beretta The type of gun James Bond carried.

Bug A microphone, radio receiver or recording device which snoops on people and listens to their conversations.

Cipher A system of disguising messages in which every letter of the alphabet is replaced by another letter, number or symbol.

Code A system of letters, figures, words or symbols which stand for other words (rather than letters) to enable secret messages to be passed.

Contact A person an agent meets, usually to pass on or receive information.

Courier An agent whose job is to pass information from headquarters to other agents, and vice versa.

Cover The false name and identity under which an agent operates.

Cryptanalysis Breaking codes and ciphers.

Cryptogram A message written in cipher.

Cryptographer Someone who transcribes messages into cipher.

Dead letter box A place where messages are left to be picked up by a contact.

Defect To change sides and work for the enemy.

Defector Someone who defects.

Dirtying Putting a room back to its normal state after it has been searched.

Double agent An agent who is employed by both

sides and is loyal to neither.

Double talk Passing messages in apparently innocent conversation by using code words. It can also mean a code in which words have alternative meanings.

Drop A place where secret messages, equipment or other items are left to be picked up by a contact.

Fix A 'put-up job' when an innocent person is made to appear to be guilty of a crime.

Fumigating Removing bugs from a room.

HQ Headquarters – the centre of the spy ring.

Ice A slang word for diamonds.

Ill Under observation by the enemy.

Lifting Removing fingerprints from an item using powder and adhesive tape.

Master spy The chief agent in a spy ring. Often no one knows his or her true identity.

Measles If someone 'has the measles' it means they are dead.

Microdot A photograph of something reduced to a single tiny dot.

Microfiche Small piece of film bearing microdots.

Microfilm Film bearing microdots.

Mole An agent working in one organization who is really employed by, and spying for, another.

Network A spy ring working in a particular area.

Nulls Extra, meaningless letters added to a cipher, often to make words the right length.

Peeper A secret agent who is good at photography.

Plant Another name for a mole, see above; also an item (e.g. incriminating evidence) deliberately placed so it will be discovered by a particular person or organization.

Postman A courier who delivers messages from one agent to another.

Put the finger on Inform against someone.

Shadow Someone who follows an agent and reports on his or her movements.

Sleeper An agent who lives in a particular place and may wait years without being used, who is called upon when needed.

Snake A flexible tube that can be poked through doors, etc., which an agent uses for listening to conversations.

Spook Another name for a spy.

Spy ring A group of spies or agents who operate together.

Sugar A bribe to get someone to do something.

Tail Another name for a shadow; to follow someone.

Voice analyser A computer that can detect inaudible changes in somebody's voice tones. By analysing these it can then tell if the person is lying.

Wireman An agent who specializes in spying by using electronic devices, such as bugs.

ANSWERS TO CODE MESSAGES AND PUZZLES

How to Disguise Yourself

1. Round your shoulders, stoop and walk bent, possibly walk with a stick.
2. Put a pebble in your shoe, or, for a stiff leg, tie a ruler behind your knee.
3. Hands. Boys' hands are usually much bigger than girls'.
4. Press your tongue against your lower front teeth.
5. Rub cocoa powder on it.
6. Draw in frown lines and put talcum powder on your hair to make it grey.

How To Tail a Suspect

The five spies circled are definitely tailing the suspect, but the others could be too!

Places From Which to Spy

Telephone kiosk
Cupboard
Curtains
Dustbin
Table
Wardrobe

How to Create Secret Codes and Ciphers

p39 **Morse code message in zig-zag**
Dinner at embassy may be poisoned –
beware.

p40 **Semaphore message**
Destroy code book immediately.

p42 **Substitution ciphers messages**
1. Collect parcel at station.
2. Meet me Tuesday in café.
3. Think they are on to me send help.

p43 **Misleading division**
Enemy flying to Paris will follow.

p44 **Phoney lasts**
Suspect M of being spy keep close watch on
him.

p44 **Back to front**
Picked up message off Internet text to
follow.

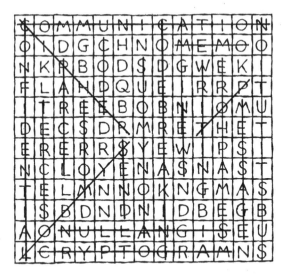

Passing Secret Messages to Your Contact

There are 6 messages hidden in the picture, and 8 differences (circled) between the two pictures.

How to Make and Use Invisible Ink

1. Honey – Eac**h one y**elled . . .
2. Vinegar – . . . **vine, Gar**y . . .
3. Lemonade, salt – Da**le**, **Mona De**nton and **Sal t**o . . .
4. Milk – E**mil**, **K**en . . .
5. Apple – . . . he**ap, ple**ase . . .
6. Potato – . . . **pot a to**mato . . .

Hiding Secret Papers and Equipment

Rebecca is the intruder. She has left a hairclip behind.

Making Your Room Proof Against Enemy Agents

Prints B and E are identical.

follow
without
being
spotted